i

For permission requests, contact:

Candid Diana Press

A division of Candid Diana LLC

www.dianawuor.com

ISBN: 979-8-9933739-0-4

First Edition, 2025

Printed in the United States of America

Edited and produced by the Candid Diana Press Team

Cover design by the Candid Diana Creative Team

Pain to Purpose Devotional

A Five-Day Reflection on Healing, Faith, and Hope

By Dr. Diana C. Awuor

Dedication

To my daughters, Kendi-Jeanne, Keana-Anaya, and Kenna-Arella —
you are my greatest joy and the reason these pages carry hope.

May you always remember:
Pain does not define you,
God's purpose refines you.

With all my love,
Mama — Dr. Diana C. Awuor

Foreword

Pain to Purpose is more than a book—it is a journey of healing and restoration. I had the privilege of experiencing it firsthand during one of Dr. Diana Awuor's "Pain to Purpose" Workshops held in Kenya in April 2025. Having walked through that session, I can confidently say this devotional is a profound and practical healing manual for anyone who has faced pain, trauma, or deep disappointment in their life journey.

Each section provides relatable, faith-based steps on how one can navigate, confront, and heal during seasons of pain and despair. The reflections are Spirit-led, offering guidance that ministers to the mind, body, and soul.

I wholeheartedly recommend this devotional to both individuals and groups. It is perfectly suited for Bible study circles, counseling sessions, or personal reflection. Pain to Purpose reminds us that hope is never lost and that no season of hardship lasts forever—because God is always with us.

Paulyn S. Waswa

Breast Cancer Thriver

Acknowledgments

This devotional is the fruit of many prayers, tears, and moments of grace. I could never have walked this journey alone.

First, I thank my Lord and Savior, Jesus Christ, who never left my side and who turned my pain into purpose. Without His presence and peace, this book would not exist.

To my beloved husband, Kennedy, whose steadfast love has been an anchor in every season.

To beautiful daughters — Kendi-Jeanne, Keana-Anaya, and Kenna-Arella — you are my joy and my daily reminder of God's goodness. Your lives inspire me to keep choosing hope.

To my mother, Pastor Mary Collette, whose prayers became my lifeline and whose faith strengthened my own.

To my siblings — Olivia, Patrick, Gloria, and Timothy — who cried with me and walked beside me through doctor visits and hospital corridors. Your presence was a gift that held me up when I could not stand on my own.

To my friend **Paulyn Waswa**, a fellow cancer thriver and believer, who stood with me in faith, believed with me, and even traveled with me to Oyugis for the *Pain to Purpose Workshop*, where we piloted this devotional to ensure it carried the impact God intended. Your courage and faith made this journey lighter.

To my friends, and prayer warriors who encouraged me with words, intercession, and presence — I am deeply grateful.

To every cancer patient and thriver who has shared their story with me and the — you are the heartbeat of this work.

Finally, to the readers holding this book: thank you for choosing to journey with me. My prayer is that as you reflect, write, and engage with these pages, you will discover that your pain, too, can be transformed into purpose.

With love,

Dr. Diana C. Awuor

Introduction

Dear friend,

Thank you for choosing to walk through this devotional. My prayer is that in the next five days, you will encounter God in a personal way as you reflect on your own story, your struggles, and the hope that only Christ can give.

When I was diagnosed with breast cancer in 2020, my world turned upside down. I was a young mother with three little girls — the oldest just six, another one-year-old, and the youngest still an infant. I was also in the middle of my doctoral studies. Life felt unbearable, and I began to question everything I believed about God.

At my lowest point, I even asked my doctors to end my life. That was how heavy the pain was. But God, in His mercy, met me there. He taught me that pain is not wasted, and that when surrendered to Him, it can become a doorway to purpose.

This devotional is born out of that journey — the tears, the doubts, the wrestling, and finally, the peace of knowing that Christ is with us in every storm. Each day, you'll read Scripture, reflect on part of my story, and be guided through questions and practices that will help you turn your own pain into purpose.

You don't have to do this journey alone. Read it by yourself, with a small group, or even with your family. Let it spark conversations, prayers, and healing.

I believe that as you go through these pages, the Lord will take what the enemy meant for harm and turn it into something good in your life (Genesis 50:20).

With love and hope,
Dr. Diana C. Awuor

Table of Contents

Dedication... iv

Foreword... v

Acknowledgments vi

Introduction... viii

DAY 1: THE PAIN IS HERE. WHAT NEXT?.. 1

Day 1 — The Pain is Here. What Next?... 2

    Scripture... 2

    My Story 3

    Reflection Questions: 4

    Prayer 8

    Write your prayer.. 8

    Write and describe one step you will take towards healing................... 9

    Memory Verse 10

    Practice This Day 10

    Notes 11

DAY 2: WHO SHOULD KNOW THERE IS PAIN 14

Day 2 — Who Should Know There Is Pain?.. 15

    Scripture... 15

    My Story 16

    Reflection Questions: 17

    Exercise.. 20

    Prayer 21

    Write your prayer... 21

    Write and describe one step you will take towards healing................. 22

    Memory Verse 23

    Practice This Day 23

    Notes 24

DAY 3: CAN I GET YOUR ATTENTION, PLEASE?............................ 27

Day 3 — Can I Get Your Attention, Please? 28

    Scripture 28

    My Story 29

    Reflection Questions: 31

    Exercise 34

    Prayer 35

    Write and describe one step you will take towards healing 36

    Memory Verse 37

    Practice This Day 37

    Notes..38

DAY 4: GOD, WHY? 41

Day 4 — God, Why? 42

    Scripture 42

    My Story 43

    Reflection Questions: 44

    Exercise 47

    Prayer 48

    Write your prayer 48

    Write and describe one step you will take towards healing 49

    Memory Verse 50

    Practice This Day 50

    Notes..51

DAY 5: PAIN LESSONS FOR CHRISTIANS 54

Day 5 — Pain Lessons for Christians 55

    Scripture 55

    My Story 56

    Reflection Questions: 57

    Exercise 60

    Prayer 61

Write your prayer.. 61

Write and describe one step you will take towards healing.......................... 62

Memory Verse 63

Practice This Day 63

Notes.. 64

What is God teaching you about pain this season? 66

List five things you are grateful for 67

Closing Prayer & Commissioning iii

About the Author iv

DAY 1: THE PAIN IS HERE. WHAT NEXT?

Day 1 — The Pain is Here. What Next?

✦ —

Scripture

> *John 16:33 (NIV) — "I have told you these things, so that in me you may have peace. In this world, you will have trouble. But take heart! I have overcome the world."*

My Story

Pain is universal. For me, it arrived violently in November 2020 with a breast cancer diagnosis. I was a young mother with a newborn in my arms, two other little girls under the age of seven, and a doctoral dissertation hanging over my head. Life was a blur of diapers, lectures, research, and sleepless nights. Cancer was not on my schedule.

When the doctor spoke the words "you have breast cancer," my mind went blank. Denial became my first refuge. Maybe the tests were wrong. Maybe the lump would vanish. Maybe God would miraculously erase it before treatment began. I prayed, fasted, bargained, and willed it to disappear. But the diagnosis remained.

As reality sank in, a different storm rose. I felt betrayed by God. How could He allow this? I was doing everything "right," serving, studying, raising my children. In my darkest moments, despair whispered that the best way to protect my children from watching me waste away was to simply end it all. I even asked my doctors if they could help me die quickly. That is how heavy the pain felt — it smothered hope and blurred my will to live.

Yet in that valley, God did not walk away. In ways I still can't fully explain, He held me together when I wanted to fall apart. He reminded me that even Jesus wrestled with fear in Gethsemane as He faced the cross. My tears did not repel Him; my questions did not offend Him. Slowly, He began to teach me that acknowledging pain is not weakness. It is the doorway to healing. Only when I named my suffering before Him could He start transforming it.

Reflection Questions:

1. What pain are you currently minimizing, denying, or trying to handle on your own?

_____

_____

_____

_____

_____

_____

_____

_____

_____

_____

_____

_____

_____

_____

_____

_____

_____

2. How does Jesus' victory in John 16:33 help you face your present reality?

_____

_____

_____

_____

_____

_____

_____

_____

_____

_____

_____

_____

_____

_____

_____

_____

_____

_____

3. What fears arise when you imagine fully accepting your situation before God?

_____

_____

_____

_____

_____

_____

_____

_____

_____

_____

_____

_____

_____

_____

_____

_____

_____

_____

Exercise

Take a quiet moment to name your pain before the Lord. If in a group, share one
sentence if comfortable. Respond together: 'We see you. Christ is with you.'

_____

_____

_____

_____

_____

_____

_____

_____

_____

_____

_____

_____

Prayer

Lord Jesus, we bring our pain to You. We confess that sometimes we try to carry it alone or push You aside. Give us strength, grace, and peace. Amen.

_____

Write your prayer

_____

_____

_____

_____

_____

_____

_____

_____

_____

_____

_____

_____

Write and describe one step you will take towards healing

_____

_____

_____

_____

_____

_____

_____

_____

_____

_____

_____

_____

_____

_____

_____

_____

_____

Memory Verse

John 16:33 — "In this world you will have trouble. But take heart! I have overcome the world."

_____

Practice This Day

Each day, pray a simple prayer of acceptance: 'Lord, I accept that

_____. Meet me here with Your peace.'

Notes

DAY 2: WHO SHOULD KNOW THERE IS PAIN

Day 2 — Who Should Know There Is Pain?

✦ —

Scripture

> *1 Peter 4:16 (NIV) — "If you suffer as a Christian, do not be ashamed, but praise God that you bear that name."*
>
> *Galatians 6:2 (NIV) — "Carry each other's burdens, and in this way you will fulfill the law of Christ."*
>
> *Romans 12:15 (NIV) — "Rejoice with those who rejoice; mourn with those who mourn."*

My Story

When I was diagnosed, I made mistakes about who I shared my pain with. Some repeated my story carelessly; others spoke words of death — telling me to "create memories" because they assumed I was going to die. Their focus was death, not life.

One sister-in-law called and said I needed to focus on "creating memories" with my family, especially my little kids. Of course, I knew what she really meant: she thought I should leave my children with memories of me for when I die of cancer. Another in-law called to say that if only I had known earlier, I should have taken out a life insurance policy. Can you imagine? What she was implying was that without life insurance, I was going to die of cancer and leave my family with nothing. Life! Why did she assume I didn't have one anyway?

But there were also safe places. My church elders and pastors prayed with me. My mother, a pastor, stood in the gap. And perhaps one of the greatest lifelines God gave me was therapy. Sitting with my therapists and psychiatrists, I was able to pour out the thoughts I couldn't share with anyone else. They were trained to hold my pain without judgment, to help me untangle the grief, fear, and anger, and to give me tools to keep going. Therapy became a sacred space where I was reminded that I was not crazy for feeling the weight I carried — I was human.

Through this I learned: not everyone should know your pain, but someone must. The body of Christ is meant to carry one another's burdens. And sometimes, God carries us through the wise counsel of trained professionals.

I also discovered the importance of protecting my circle. Some friends distanced themselves because they didn't want the sadness every time we spoke. And that's okay. Pain teaches you who is truly called to walk with you in the valley — and who cannot. The right circle, and the right professionals, can be the difference between drowning in despair and learning to breathe again.

Reflection Questions:

4. Where has shame kept you silent about your struggles?

_____

_____

_____

_____

_____

_____

_____

_____

_____

_____

_____

_____

_____

_____

_____

_____

_____

_____

5. Who are the trustworthy, faith-filled people you can lean on?

_____

_____

_____

_____

_____

_____

_____

_____

_____

_____

_____

_____

_____

_____

_____

_____

_____

_____

6. What boundaries might you need to put in place as you share your story?

_____

_____

_____

_____

_____

_____

_____

_____

_____

_____

_____

_____

_____

_____

_____

_____

_____

Exercise

Draw a circle with three rings: Inner, Trusted, Acquaintances. Place names accordingly. Pray for courage and wisdom.

Prayer

Lord, give me courage to open up to the right people and wisdom to set boundaries. Surround me with those who will lift me up. Amen.

_____

Write your prayer

_____

_____

_____

_____

_____

_____

_____

_____

_____

_____

_____

_____

Write and describe one step you will take towards healing

_____

_____

_____

_____

_____

_____

_____

_____

_____

_____

_____

_____

_____

_____

_____

_____

_____

Memory Verse

Galatians 6:2 — "Carry each other's burdens, and in this way you will fulfill the law of Christ."

Practice This Day

Tell one safe person: 'I'm carrying _____. Would you pray with me this week?'

Notes

DAY 3: CAN I GET YOUR ATTENTION, PLEASE?

Day 3 — Can I Get Your Attention, Please?

— ✦ —

Scripture

Psalm 46:10 (NIV) — "Be still, and know that I am God."

My Story

After speaking to the right people and building a circle of prayer warriors I called my pace setters, the Lord shifted me into a season of stillness. He reminded me of His word: "Be still, and know that I am God."

In that quiet place, Scripture became more than words on a page — it was as if God was writing personal letters to me. Like Jacob, I wrestled with Him in prayer. I asked questions, I demanded answers, and I even pleaded with Him for three clear signs that He was still with me. He gave me all three.

One of the most unforgettable moments came when a brother named Daniel prayed over me. Without knowing my hidden request, he asked God specifically to restore my joy. In that moment, I knew heaven had heard me because I urgently needed my joy back. And if you've interacted with me since then, perhaps you've noticed how joyful I've become. Joy, I've learned, is far greater than happiness — happiness shifts with circumstances, but joy is anchored in God's presence. The Lord granted me His joy, and it has carried me ever since.

Allow me to share one prayer style that lifted my supplication to another level. My dear friend, Carolyne Kiplangat — who has no idea how much of an influence she has been on me — taught me to return God's promises back to Him in prayer, to literally table His Word before Him. She also encouraged me to try the ACTS formula:

A for Adoration — begin with worship, because He is worthy.

C for Confession — because we all fall short, and cleansing our hearts matters.

T for Thanksgiving — for His past mercies and faithfulness, before we ask for more.

S for Supplication — only then do we bring our requests before Him.

This framework transformed my conversations with God. It gave structure to my cries in the darkest seasons, and it taught me to focus on who He is before what I need.

I encourage you to try this formula. It brings a holy ease to prayer, especially when your soul feels too weak to find words.

Reflection Questions:

7. What are you trying to control that God is asking you to surrender?

_____

_____

_____

_____

_____

_____

_____

_____

_____

_____

_____

_____

_____

_____

_____

_____

8. How might you create space for stillness this week?

_____

_____

_____

_____

_____

_____

_____

_____

_____

_____

_____

_____

_____

_____

_____

_____

_____

_____

9. Recall a time God spoke to you unexpectedly. What did you learn?

_____

_____

_____

_____

_____

_____

_____

_____

_____

_____

_____

_____

_____

_____

_____

_____

_____

Exercise

Spend five minutes in silence. Write down what God brings to mind. Make a 'letting go' list.

_____

_____

_____

_____

_____

_____

_____

_____

_____

_____

_____

_____

_____

_____

Prayer

Lord, help me quiet my heart and hear Your voice. Teach me to surrender and rest in You. Amen.

_____

Write your prayer

Write and describe one step you will take towards healing

_____

_____

_____

_____

_____

_____

_____

_____

_____

_____

_____

_____

_____

_____

_____

_____

_____

Memory Verse

Psalm 46:10 — "Be still, and know that I am God."

Practice This Day

Spend five minutes daily in silence. Pray: 'Speak, Lord; Your servant is listening.'

Notes

DAY 4: GOD, WHY?

Day 4 — God, Why?

— ✦ —

Scripture

Genesis 50:20 (NIV) — "You intended to harm me, but God intended it for good to accomplish what is now being done, the saving of many lives."

Romans 8:28 (NIV) — "And we know that in all things God works for the good of those who love him, who have been called according to his purpose."

My Story

When cancer came, my first cry was, "God, why?" At one point, I even refused to eat what I was advised to eat — not out of despair, but because I believed that salmon and organic chicken were part of the "animal meats" that had caused the diagnosis in the first place. I lacked knowledge.

I knew I had the sickle cell trait, but I had no idea how much it was contributing to my unstable blood levels during treatment. Half of my red blood cells were already sickled, and without certain foods to sustain me, my body could not endure the harshness of chemotherapy drugs like Carboplatin. After I missed chemotherapy twice because my levels were too low, I finally listened. I began eating salmon, omena, and organic chicken — and my blood levels came back up and remained stable.

That was a turning point. I began to understand that some white meats, when chosen carefully, could actually strengthen me through treatment. Food was no longer the enemy — it was part of God's provision for healing. I learned that each person's body and case is different, and that understanding our bodies and what they require is essential in treatment and even post-treatment.

It was amazing how God used this lesson. Around that same time, my mother shared with me about a friend who had died from cervical cancer. She hadn't been able to afford the recommended foods, nor did she have access to oncology dieticians. That broke me — and it was in that very moment that God whispered my assignment: "Feed My people."

I began by providing nutritious meals for poor cancer patients. Later, He expanded my assignment beyond food to awareness, education, and international speaking. My work shifted from foodbanks to global platforms. Today, I feed not just bodies but minds — sharing the knowledge that saves lives.

Scripture says, "My people perish for lack of knowledge." (Hosea 4:6). The question "Why?" turned into a testimony. My pain became the seed for my purpose.

Reflection Questions:

10. What loss or betrayal caused you to ask, 'Why, God?'

_____

_____

_____

_____

_____

_____

_____

_____

_____

_____

_____

_____

_____

_____

_____

_____

11. How has wise counsel shifted your perspective?

_____

_____

_____

_____

_____

_____

_____

_____

_____

_____

_____

_____

_____

_____

_____

_____

_____

12. Where might your pain intersect with someone else's need?

_____

_____

_____

_____

_____

_____

_____

_____

_____

_____

_____

_____

_____

_____

_____

_____

Exercise

Pair up with a friend or journal privately: name one way your story could bless another person this week.

_____

_____

_____

_____

_____

_____

_____

_____

_____

_____

_____

_____

_____

_____

Prayer

God, I bring my 'whys' to You. I may not have all the answers,
but I trust Your purpose. Let my story bless others. Amen.

Write your prayer

_____

_____

_____

_____

_____

_____

_____

_____

_____

_____

_____

Write and describe one step you will take towards healing

_____

_____

_____

_____

_____

_____

_____

_____

_____

_____

_____

_____

_____

_____

_____

_____

Memory Verse

Romans 8:28 — "And we know that in all things God works for the good of those who love him, who have been called according to his purpose."

Practice This Day

Do one tangible act of service that flows from your story. Notice how God uses it.

Notes

DAY 5: PAIN LESSONS FOR CHRISTIANS

Day 5 — Pain Lessons for Christians

— ✦ —

Scripture

Ecclesiastes 2:23 (NIV) — "All their days their work is grief and pain; even at night their minds do not rest. This too is meaningless."

Ephesians 1:11 (NIV) — "In him we were also chosen, having been predestined according to the plan of him who works out everything in conformity with the purpose of his will."

2 Corinthians 12:9 (NIV) — "But he said to me, 'My grace is sufficient for you, for my power is made perfect in weakness.'"

My Story

Through breast cancer, I learned that pain is never wasted. It reminded me that life is fragile, taught me to rely on God, and opened doors I never imagined. From feeding patients to speaking internationally, my pain became my platform. Today I carry a message of hope: there is life after diagnosis, and purpose beyond suffering.

Reflection Questions:

13. Which of these lessons speaks most to your current season?

_____

_____

_____

_____

_____

_____

_____

_____

_____

_____

_____

_____

_____

_____

_____

_____

14. How has God already used your pain for His glory?

_____

_____

_____

_____

_____

_____

_____

_____

_____

_____

_____

_____

_____

_____

_____

_____

_____

15. What step can you take to live with gratitude in the midst of suffering?

_____

_____

_____

_____

_____

_____

_____

_____

_____

_____

_____

_____

_____

_____

_____

_____

_____

Exercise

Craft a simple 'rule of life' for the next month — prayer, Scripture, rest, fellowship, and service. Share with a friend.

_____

_____

_____

_____

_____

_____

_____

_____

_____

_____

_____

_____

_____

Prayer

Sovereign Lord, thank You that You never waste our pain.
Shape us for Your glory. May our lives point others to Your
goodness. Amen.

_____

Write your prayer

_____

_____

_____

_____

_____

_____

_____

_____

_____

_____

_____

_____

_____

Write and describe one step you will take towards healing

_____

_____

_____

_____

_____

_____

_____

_____

_____

_____

_____

_____

_____

_____

_____

_____

_____

Memory Verse

Ephesians 1:11 — "In him we were also chosen, having been predestined according to the plan of him who works out everything in conformity with the purpose of his will."

Practice This Day

Live out your 'rule of life' for 30 days. Notice how God meets you in each rhythm, and share your testimony.

Notes

What is God teaching you about pain this season?

_____

_____

_____

_____

_____

_____

_____

_____

_____

_____

_____

_____

_____

_____

_____

_____

_____

List five things you are grateful for

_____

_____

_____

_____

_____

_____

_____

_____

_____

_____

_____

_____

_____

_____

_____

_____

_____

"Your pain does not define you;

God's purpose refines you"

Closing Prayer & Commissioning

Lord Almighty,

We thank You because You waste nothing. You take our tears and turn them into seeds, You take our pain and transform it into purpose. Bless each reader. May their scars become testimonies of grace. Send them forth as carriers of hope. In Jesus' name, Amen.

About the Author

Dr. Diana C. Awuor is a breast cancer thriver, international speaker, Fulbright Scholar, and Presidential Lifetime Achievement Award honoree. Diagnosed with breast cancer in 2020 while balancing motherhood, doctoral studies, and ministry, she turned her journey of pain into a message of resilience and faith.

She is the founder of Pain to Purpose, a global initiative empowering individuals to transform trauma into testimony. Formerly providing meals for cancer patients, she now focuses on awareness, education, and international advocacy, pointing patients to existing services while spreading hope worldwide.

Dr. Awuor is also an author, higher education professional, accessibility specialist, philanthropist, and entrepreneur. Through her story, she continues to inspire countless people to believe that with God, even pain can be transformed into purpose.

www.ingramcontent.com/pod-product-compliance
Lightning Source LLC
Chambersburg PA
CBHW081140090426
42736CB00018B/3427